BEST SONGS AND BALLADS OF OLD IRELAND

Compiled by

Mary McGarry

Cover illustration by RICHARD HOOK

WOLFE PUBLISHING LTD
10 EARLHAM STREET LONDON WC2

30p

Also by Wolfe Publishing:

The Lively Ghosts of Ireland
by Hans Holzer

Best Irish Ghostly Tales
Compiled by Mary McGarry

The Book of Blarney
by Anthony Butler

Best Irish Songs
by Percy French
Edited with an Introduction by Tony Butler

Best Irish Jokes
by Tony Butler

More Best Irish Jokes
by Tony Butler

Best Irish Limericks
by Tony Butler

Best Ulster Jokes
by Ken Nixon

Great Folk Tales of Old Ireland
Compiled by Mary McGarry

Great Fairy Tales of Ireland
Compiled by Mary McGarry

Years of the Shamrock
Edited by David Marcus

ISBN 7234 0413 5

©Wolfe Publishing Ltd., 1972, Reprinted 1974

Printed at The Grange Press, Southwick, Sussex

CONTENTS

(continued overleaf)

CONTENTS *(continued)*

INTRODUCTION

IN RECENT YEARS ballads have gained increasing popularity with both young and old alike. This in itself justifies a collection of some of Ireland's own songs. In the somewhat limited scope of a short book, I have tried to bring together as wide a variety of songs and ballads as possible, embracing a great deal of the better known works passed down through the generations.

Many of Ireland's earliest ballads were written naturally in Irish and we are indebted to men like James Clarence Mangan for his translations into English of the fine *Roisin Dubh* and others. Both 'Roisin Dubh' and the 'Dark Rosaleen' of another ballad in this book are assumed names for Ireland in an age when poets feared to speak openly of their homeland. *John O'Dwyer of the Glen* tells of the plight of the Irish rebel fleeing from the English conquerer.

The rising of 1798 left an indelible mark not only on the history of Ireland but also on its bardic community. Ballads like *Boulavogue*, *Kelly of Killann* and *Memory of the Dead* are well known by all patriots, and their fire lives on to this day, so that they are far from having a hollow ring even in 1972.

In a lighter vein there are two well-known ballads about our national emblem, the shamrock, which remains forever green in *The Dear Little Shamrock* and *The Wearin' o' the Green*. More Irish humour comes through in the colloquial ditty of *The Peeler and the Goat*, which takes a snide yet witty dig at Sir Robert Peel's protégés at work in Ireland.

I have also tried to give a taste of varying parts of the country as in *The Bells of Shandon* of Cork City, or *The Hills of Connemara* by John Keegan Casey, better known as 'Leo'. *The Rose of Tralee* and *Danny Boy* are so well loved that their inclusion needs no explanation. The Dublin street song *Cockles and Mussels* comes readily to lips all the world over, whether they be Irish or not.

For their sheer poetic and melodic quality I felt I could not overlook some of the works of Thomas Moore. His description of the magnificent *Meeting of the Waters* at the Vale of Avoca is perhaps only matched by the triumphal simplicity of *The Minstrel-Boy* or subjective thought of some of the lines of *Oft in the Stilly Night*.

However no collection such as this would be complete without at least a sample of the songs of the inimitable Percy French. Few have managed to capture the unique flavour of Irish life as French did in cheerful airs such as *Are Ye Right There, Michael?* or *Whistlin' Phil McHugh*. From his experiences on the west Clare railway to his feelings about the mountains of Mourne he brings the same light yet ingenious touch that has given his work a place and popularity all its own.

There has been much rewriting of songs and so-called modernisation of the ballad theme, but the songs and ballads in this collection are chosen for their originality of treatment and sincerity of thought. There is a growing number of people who feel that these represent the real Ireland of historical and literary fame. Of course one cannot hope to satisfy everybody all the time but in this selection of the favourites of a great many Irish people, myself included, I am sure the reader will find many that appeal to him personally and quite a few that will return easily to his mind and his lips.

THE MINSTREL-BOY

Thomas Moore

The Minstrel-Boy to the war is gone,
    In the ranks of death you'll find him;
His father's sword he has girded on,
    And his wild harp slung behind him.
'Land of song!' said the warrior-bard,
    'Tho' all the world betrays thee,
One sword, at least, thy rights shall guard,
    One faithful harp shall praise thee!'

The Minstrel fell! – but the foeman's chain
    Could not bring his proud soul under;
The harp he loved ne'er spoke again,
    For he tore its chords asunder;
And said, 'No chains shall sully thee,
    Thou soul of love and bravery!
Thy songs were made for the pure and free,
    They shall never sound in slavery.'

ROISIN DUBH

James Clarence Mangan

O, bitter woe, that we must go, across the sea!
O, grief of griefs, that Lords and Chiefs, their homes must flee!
A tyrant band o'erruns the land, this land so green,
And, though we grieve, we still must leave, our Dark Roisin!

My darling Dove, my Life, my Love, to me so dear,
Once torn apart from you, my heart will break, I fear,
O, golden Flower of Beauty's bower! O radiant Queen!
I mourn in bonds; my soul desponds; my Dark Roisin!

In hope and joy, while yet a boy, I wooed my bride;
I sought not pelf; I sought herself and naught beside,
My health is flown, 'tis old I'm grown; and though I ween,
My heart will break, I must forsake my Dark Roisin!

The fairest fair you ever were, the peerless Maid;
For bards and priests your daily feasts were richly laid.
Amid my dole, on you my soul still loves to lean,
Though I must brave the stormy wave, my Dark Roisin!

In years gone by, how you and I seemed glad and blest!
My wedded wife, you cheered my life, you warmed my breast!
The fairest one the living sun o'er decked with sheen,
The brightest rose that buds or blows, is Dark Roisin!

My guiding Star of Hope you are, all glow and grace,
My blooming Love, my Spouse above all Adam's race;
In deed or thought you cherish naught of low or mean;
The base alone can hate my own – my Dark Roisin!

O, never mourn as one forlorn, but bide your hour;
Your friends ere long, combined and strong, will prove their
power,
From distant Spain will sail a train to change the scene
That makes you sad, for one more glad, my Dark Roisin!

Till then, adieu! my Fond and True! adieu, till then!
Though now you grieve, still, still believe we'll meet again;
I'll yet return, with hopes that burn, and broad-sword keen;
Fear not, nor think you e'er can sink, my Dark Roisin!

THE BELLS OF SHANDON

Francis Sylvester Mahony (Father Prout)

With deep affection
And recollection
I often think of
        Those Shandon bells
Whose sounds so wild would,
In the days of childhood,
Fling round my cradle
        Their magic spells.
On this I ponder
Where'er I wander,
And thus grow fonder
        Sweet Cork, of thee;
With thy bells of Shandon,
That sound so grand on
The pleasant waters
        Of the river Lee.

I've heard bells chiming
Full many a clime in,
Tolling sublime in
        Cathedral Shrine,
While at a glib rate
Brass tongues would vibrate
But all their music
        Spoke nought like thine:
For memory dwelling
On each proud swelling
Of the belfry knelling
        Its bold notes free
Made the bells of Shandon
Sound far more grand on
The pleasant waters
        Of the river Lee.

I've heard bells tolling
Old 'Adrian's Mole' in,
Their thunder rolling
        From the Vatican,
And cymbals glorious
Swinging uproarious
In the gorgeous turrets
        Of Notre Dame;
But thy sounds were sweeter
Than the dome of Peter
Flings o'er the Tiber,
        Pealing solemnly;
Oh, the bells of Shandon
Sound far more grand on
The pleasant waters
        Of the river Lee.

There's a bell in Moscow,
While on tower and kiosk O;
In Saint Sophia
        The Turkman gets,
And loud in air
Calls men to prayer
From the tapering summit
        Of tall minarets,
Such empty phantom
I freely grant them;
But there's an anthem
        More dear to me –
'Tis the bells of Shandon
That sound so grand on
The pleasant waters
        Of the river Lee.

'ARE YE RIGHT THERE, MICHAEL?'

A Lay of the Wild West Clare by Percy French

You may talk of Columbus's sailing
Across the Atlantical sea
But he never tried to go railing
From Ennis as far as Kilkee.
You run for the train in the mornin',
The excursion train starting at eight,
You're there when the clock gives the warnin',
And there for an hour you'll wait.

SPOKEN

And as you're waiting in the train,
You'll hear the guard sing this refrain:

> *'Are ye right there, Michael? are ye right?*
> *Do you think that we'll be there before the night?*
> *Ye've been so long in startin',*
> *That ye couldn't say for sartin' –*
> *Still ye might now, Michael, so ye might!'*

They find out where the engine's been hiding,
And it drags you to sweet Corofin;
Sez the guard, 'Back her down on the siding,
There's the goods from Kilrush comin' in'.
Perhaps it comes in in two hours,
Perhaps it breaks down on the way:
'If it does', sez the guard, 'be the powers,
We're here for the rest of the day!'

And while you sit and curse your luck,
The train backs down into a truck!

> *'Are ye right there, Michael, are ye right?*
> *Have ye got the parcel there for Mrs. White?*
> *Ye haven't! Oh, begorra!*
> *Say it's comin' down to-morra –*
> *And it might now, Michael, so it might!'*

At Lahinch the sea shines like a jewel,
With joy you are ready to shout,
When the stoker cries out, 'There's no fuel,
And the fire's taytotally out.
But hand up that bit of a log there –
I'll soon have ye out of the fix;
There's a fine clamp of turf in the bog there';
And the rest go a-gatherin' sticks.

And while you're breakin' bits of trees,
You hear some wise remarks like these:

> *'Are ye right there, Michael, are ye right?*
> *Do you think you can get the fire to light?'*
> *'Oh, an hour you'll require,*
> *For the turf it might be drier –'*
> *'Well it might now, Michael, so it might!'*

Kilkee! Oh, you never get near it!
You're in luck if the train brings you back,
For the permanent way is so queer, it
Spends most of its time off the track.
Uphill the ould engin' is climbin',

While passengers push with a will;
You're in luck when you reach Ennistymon
For all the way home is down-hill.

SPOKEN

And as you're wobbling through the dark,
You hear the guard make this remark:

> '*Are ye right there, Michael, are ye right?*
> *Do ye think that we'll be home before it's light?*'
> ' *'Tis all dependin' whether*
> *The ould engin' howlds together –*'
> '*And it might now, Michael, so it might!*'

DARK ROSALEEN

James Clarence Mangan

O, my Dark Rosaleen,
Do not sigh, do not weep!
The priests are on the ocean green,
They march along the Deep.
There's wine . . . from the royal Pope,
Upon the ocean green;
And Spanish ale shall give you hope,
My Dark Rosaleen!
My Dark Rosaleen!
Shall glad your heart, shall give you hope,
Shall give you health, and help, and hope,
My Dark Rosaleen!

Over hills, and through dales,
Have I roamed for your sake;
All yesterday I sailed with sails
On river and on lake.
The Erne . . . at its highest flood,
I dashed across unseen,
For there was lightning in my blood,
My Dark Rosaleen!
My own Rosaleen!
Oh! there was lightning in my blood,
Red lightning lightened through my blood,
My Dark Rosaleen!

All day long, in unrest,
To and fro do I move.
The very soul within my breast
Is wasted for you, love!
The heart . . . in my bosom faints
To think of you, my Queen,
My life of life, my saint of saints,
My Dark Rosaleen!
My Own Rosaleen!
To hear your sweet and sad complaints,
My life, my love, my saint of saints,
My Dark Rosaleen!

Woe and pain, pain and woe,
Are my lot night and noon,
To see your bright face clouded so,
Like to the mournful moon.
But yet . . . will I rear your throne
Again in golden sheen;
'Tis you shall reign, shall reign alone,
My Dark Rosaleen,

My own Rosaleen!
'Tis you shall have the golden throne,
'Tis you shall reign, and reign alone,
My Dark Rosaleen!

Over dews, over sands,
Will I fly, for your weal;
Your holy delicate white hands
Shall girdle me with steel
At home . . . in your emerald bowers,
From morning's dawn till e'en,
You'll pray for me, my flower of flowers,
My Dark Rosaleen!
My fond Rosaleen!
You'll think of me through daylight's hours,
My virgin flower, my flower of flowers,
My Dark Rosaleen!

I could scale the blue air,
I could plough the high hills,
Oh, I could kneel all night in prayer,
To heal your many ills!
And one . . . beamy smile from you
Would float like light between
My toils and me, my own, my true,
My Dark Rosaleen!
My fond Rosaleen!
Would give me life and soul anew,
A second life, a soul anew,
My Dark Rosaleen!

O! the Erne shall run red
With redundance of blood,
The earth shall rock beneath our tread,

And flames wrap hill and wood,
And gun-peal, and slogan cry,
Wake many a glen serene.
Ere you shall fade, ere you shall die,
My Dark Rosaleen!
My own Rosaleen!
The Judgement Hour must first be nigh,
Ere you can fade, ere you can die,
My Dark Rosaleen.

THE DEAR LITTLE SHAMROCK

Andrew Cherry

There's a dear little plant that grows in our isle,
'Twas St. Patrick himself, sure, that set it;
And the sun on his labour with pleasure did smile,
And with dew from his eye often wet it.
It thrives through the bog, through the brake and the mireland,
And he called it the dear little shamrock of Ireland.
The sweet little shamrock, the dear little shamrock,
The sweet little, green little shamrock of Ireland.

The dear little plant still grows in our land,
Fresh and fair as the daughters of Erin,
Whose smiles can bewitch and whose eyes can command
In each climate that they may appear in;
And they shine through the bog, through the brake and the
mireland,
Just like their own dear little shamrock,

The sweet little shamrock, the dear little shamrock,
The sweet little, green little shamrock of Ireland.

This dear little plant that springs from our soil,
When its three little leaves are extended,
Denotes from one stem we together should toil,
And ourselves by ourselves be befriended;
And still through the bog, through the brake and the mireland
From one root should branch like the shamrock of Ireland,
The sweet little shamrock, the dear little shamrock,
The sweet little, green little shamrock of Ireland.

THE MARCH TO KINSALE

Aubrey T. de Vere

O'er many a river bridged with ice,
Through many a vale with snowdrifts dumb,
Past quaking fen and precipice
The Princes of the North are come!
Lo, these are they that year by year
Roll'd back the tide of England's war;
Rejoice Kinsale! thy help is near!
That wondrous winter march is o'er.
And thus they sang, 'Tomorrow morn
Our eyes shall rest upon the foe:
Roll on, swift night, in silence borne,
And blow, thou breeze of sunrise, blow!'

Blithe as a boy on march'd the host,
With droning pipe and clear-voiced harp;
At last above that southern coast
Rang out their war steed's whinny sharp:

And up the sea-salt slopes they wound,
And airs once more of ocean quaff'd;
Those frosty woods the rocks that crown'd
As though May touch'd them waved and laugh'd.
And thus they sang, 'Tomorrow morn
Our eyes shall rest upon the foe:
Roll on, swift night, in silence borne,
And blow, thou breeze of sunrise, blow!'

Beside their watch-fires couch'd all night
Some slept, some laugh'd, at cards some play'd,
While, chaunting on a central height
Of moonlit crag, the priesthood pray'd:
And some to sweetheart, some to wife
Sent message kind; while others told
Triumphant tales of recent fight,
Or legends of their sires of old.
And thus they sang, 'Tomorrow morn
Our eyes at last shall see the foe:
Roll on, swift night, in silence borne,
And blow, thou breeze of sunrise, blow!'

BELIEVE ME, IF ALL THOSE ENDEARING YOUNG CHARMS

Thomas Moore

Believe me, if all those endearing young charms,
    Which I gaze on so fondly to-day,

Were to change by to-morrow, and fleet in my arms,
    Like fairy-gifts fading away,
Thou wouldst still be adored, as this moment thou art,
    Let thy loveliness fade as it will,
And around the dear ruin each wish of my heart
    Would entwine itself verdantly still.

It is not while beauty and youth are thine own,
    And thy cheeks unprofaned by a tear,
That the fervour and faith of a soul can be known,
    To which time will but make thee more dear;
No, the heart that has truly loved never forgets,
    But as truly loves on to the close,
As the sun-flower turns on her god, when he sets,
    The same look which she turned when he rose.

THE HILLS OF CONNEMARA

John Keegan Casey ('Leo')

The night mist thickens o'er the town,
The twilight's paling glimmers,
And through the chill, hum-laden air
The gaslight faintly shimmers.
In exile here I sit and think
My heart surcharged in sorrow,
Of home and friends that watch for me,
On the hills of Connemara;
    Those glorious hills!
    Those kindly hills!
The hills of Connemara.

The night mist thickens o'er the town,
But heavier mists are falling
On the Irish breast, bereft of love,
For peace and rest long calling,
Alone! alone! where millions throng,
As if my brain to harrow
With golden dreams of thundering streams,
On the hills of Connemara;
    The loving hills,
    The wild-eyed hills,
The hills of Connemara.

On Corrib's cheeks the moonlight sleeps,
The curragh skims full lithely;
O'er Clifden's slopes our moonlight girls
Now wander, singing blithely;
And I must bear this strife and din,
While memory strives to borrow
One look of love, one sparkling glance
Of the hills of Connemara;
    O soft-faced hills –
    O brown-tipped hills –
Brave hills of Connemara!

God's dearest blessings dwell with them,
God bless the race they foster,
If Ireland's sons were all as true,
We never would have lost her.
God prosper all my hopes,
The hopes to crown to-morrow,
When the streams will sing my welcome back
To the hills of Connemara;
    My native hills,
    My childhood hills,
The hills of Connemara.

THE SHAN VAN VOCHT

Traditional

Oh! the French are on the sea,
Says the Shan Van Vocht;
The French are on the sea,
Says the Shan Van Vocht:
Oh! the French are in the Bay,
They'll be here without delay,
And the Orange will decay,
Says the Shan Van Vocht.
Oh! the French are in the Bay,
They'll be here by break of day,
And the Orange will decay,
Says the Shan Van Vocht.

And where will they have their camp?
Says the Shan Van Vocht;
Where will they have their camp?
Says the Shan Van Vocht;
On the Curragh of Kildare,
The boys they will be there,
With their pikes in good repair,
Says the Shan Van Vocht.
To the Curragh of Kildare,
The boys they will repair,
And Lord Edward will be there,
Says the Shan Van Vocht.

Then what will the yeomen do?
Says the Shan Van Vocht;
What will the yeomen do?

Says the Shan Van Vocht;
What should the yeomen do,
But throw off the Red and Blue,
And swear that they'll be true
To the Shan Van Vocht?
What should the yeomen do
But throw off the red and blue,
And swear that they'll be true
To the Shan Van Vocht?

THE MOUNTAINS OF MOURNE

Percy French

Oh, Mary, this London's a wonderful sight,
Wid the people here workin' by day and by night:
They don't sow potatoes, nor barley, nor wheat,
But there's gangs o' them diggin' for gold in the street –
At least, when I axed them, that's what I was told,
So I just took a hand at this diggin' for gold.
But for all that I found there, I might as well be
Where the Mountains o' Mourne sweep down to the sea.

I believe that, when writin', a wish you expressed
As to how the fine ladies in London were dressed.
Well, if you'll believe me, when axed to a ball,
They don't wear a top to their dresses at all!

Oh, I've seen them myself, and you could not, in thrath,
Say if they were bound for a ball or a bath –
Don't be startin' them fashions now, Mary Machree,
Where the Mountains o' Mourne sweep down to the sea.

I seen England's King from the top of a bus –
I never knew him, though he means to know us:
And though by the Saxon we once were oppressed,
Still, I cheered – God forgive me – I cheered wid the rest,
And now that he's visited Erin's green shore,
We'll be much better friends than we've been heretofore,
When we've got all we want, we're as quiet as can be
Where the Mountains o' Mourne sweep down to the sea.

You remember young Peter O'Loughlin, of course –
Well, here he is now at the head o' the Force.
I met him to-day, I was crossin' the Strand,
And he stopped the whole street wid wan wave of his hand:
And there we stood talking of days that are gone,
While the whole population of London looked on;
But for all these great powers, he's wishful like me,
To be back where dark Mourne sweeps down to the sea.

There's beautiful girls here – oh, never mind!
With beautiful shapes Nature never designed,
And lovely complexions, all roses and crame,
But O'Loughlin remarked wid regard to them same:
'That if at those roses you venture to sip,
The colour might all come away on your lip',
So I'll wait for the wild rose that's waitin' for me –
Where the Mountains o' Mourne sweep down to the sea.

JACKETS GREEN

Michael Scanlan

When I was a maiden fair and young,
On the pleasant banks of Lee,
No bird that in the greenwood sung
Was half so blithe and free.
My heart ne'er beat with flying feet,
No love sang me her queen,
Till down the glen rode Sarsfield's men,
And they wore the jackets green.

Young Donal sat on his gallant grey
Like a king on a royal seat,
And my heart leapt out on his regal way,
To worship at his feet.
Oh! love, had you come in those colours dressed,
And wooed with a soldier's mien,
I'd have laid my head on your throbbing breast
For the sake of your jacket green.

No hoarded wealth did my love own,
Save the good sword that he bore,
But I loved him for himself alone,
And the colours bright he wore;
For had he come in England's red,
To make me England's queen,
I'd rove the high green hills instead,
For the sake of the Irish green.

When William stormed with shot and shell,
At the walls of Garryowen,

In the breach of death my Donal fell,
And he sleeps near the Treaty Stone;
That breach the foeman never crossed,
While he swung his broadsword keen
But I do not weep my darling lost,
For he fell in his jacket green.

When Sarsfield sailed away I wept
As I heard the wild ochone,
I felt, then, dead as the men who slept
'Neath the fields of Garryowen –
While Ireland held my Donal blessed,
And no wild sea rolled between,
Till I would fold him to my breast,
All robed in his Irish green.

My soul has sobbed like waves of woe,
That sad o'er tombstones break,
For I buried my heart in his grave below,
For his and for Ireland's sake.
And I cry, 'Make way for the soldier's bride,
In your halls of death, sad queen,'
For I long to rest by my true love's side,
And wrapped in the folds of green.

I saw the Shannon's purple tide
Roll by the Irish town,
As I stood in the breach by Donal's side,
When England's flag went down.
And now it glowers as it seeks the skies,
Like a blood-red curse between,
I weep, but 'tis not women's sighs
That will raise the Irish Green.

Oh! Ireland, sad is thy lonely soul,
And loud beats the winter sea,
But sadder and higher the wild waves roll
From the hearts that break for thee.
Yet grief shall come to our heartless foes,
And their thrones in the dust be seen,
But Irish maids love none but those
Who wear the jackets green.

COCKLES AND MUSSELS

Traditional

In Dublin's fair city
Where the girls are so pretty
I first set my eyes on sweet Molly Malone
As she wheeled her wheelbarrow
Through streets broad and narrow
Crying, 'Cockles and mussels, alive, alive-oh!'

CHORUS:
> Alive, alive-oh!
> Alive, alive-oh!
> Crying 'Cockles and mussels, alive, alive-oh!'

She was a fishmonger
And sure 'twas no wonder,
For so were her father and mother before:
And they both wheeled their barrows
Through streets broad and narrow
Crying 'Cockles and mussels, alive, alive-oh!'

CHORUS

She died of a fever
And no one could save her,
And that was the end of sweet Molly Malone;
And her ghost wheels her barrow
Through streets broad and narrow
Crying, 'Cockles and mussels, alive, alive-oh!'

CHORUS

JOHN O'DWYER OF THE GLEN

Thomas Furlong

Blithe the bright dawn found me,
Rest with strength had crown'd me,
Sweet the birds sung round me,
Sport was all their toil.
The horn its clang was keeping,
Forth the fox was creeping,
Round each dame stood weeping
O'er that prowler's spoil.
Hark! the foe is calling,
Fast the woods are falling,
Scenes and sights appalling
Mark the wasted soil.

War and confiscation
Curse the fallen nation;
Gloom and desolation
Shade the lost land o'er.

Chill the winds are blowing,
Death aloft is going;
Peace or hope seems growing
For our race no more.
Hark! the foe is calling,
Fast the woods are falling,
Scenes and sights appalling
Throng our blood-stained shore.

Where's my goat to cheer me?
Now it plays not near me;
Friends no more can hear me;
Strangers round me stand.
Nobles once high-hearted,
From their homes have parted,
Scatter'd scared, and startled
By a base-born band.
Hark! the foe is calling,
Fast the woods are falling,
Scenes and sights appalling
Thicken round the land.

Oh! that death had found me,
And in darkness bound me,
Ere each object round me
Grew so sweet, so dear.
Spots that once were cheering,
Girls beloved, endearing,
Friends from whom I'm steering,
Take this parting tear.
Hark! the foe is calling,
Fast the woods are falling,
Scenes and sights appalling
Plague and haunt me here.

THE MEETING OF THE WATERS

Thomas Moore

There is not in the wide world a valley so sweet
As that vale in whose bosom the bright waters meet;
Oh! the last rays of feeling and life must depart,
Ere the bloom of that valley shall fade from my heart.

Yet it was not that Nature had shed o'er the scene
Her purest of crystal and brightest of green;
'Twas not her soft magic of streamlet or hill,
Oh! no, – it was something more exquisite still.

'Twas that friends, the beloved of my bosom, were near,
Who made every dear scene of enchantment more dear,
And who felt how the best charms of Nature improve,
When we see them reflected from looks that we love.

Sweet vale of Avoca! how calm could I rest
In thy bosom of shade, with the friends I love best,
Where the storms that we feel in this cold world should cease,
And our hearts, like thy waters, be mingled in peace.

THE CROPPY BOY

Traditional

It was very early in the Spring,
The birds did whistle and sweetly sing,
Changing their notes from tree to tree,
And the song they sang was Old Ireland free.

It was early in the night
The yeomen cavalry gave me a fright;
The yeomen cavalry was my downfall
And taken was I by Lord Cornwall.

'Twas in the guard-house where I was laid
And in a parlour where I was tried;
My sentence passed and my courage low
When to Dungannon I was forced to go.

As I was passing by my father's door,
My brother William stood at the door;
My aged father stood at the door;
And my tender mother her hair she tore.

As I was walking up Wexford Street
My own first counsin I chanced to meet:
My own first cousin did me betray,
And for one bare guinea swore my life away.

My sister Mary heard the express,
She ran upstairs in her mourning dress –
Five hundred guineas I will lay down,
To see my brother through Wexford town.

As I was walking up Wexford Hill,
Who could blame me to cry my fill?
I looked behind and I looked before,
But my tender mother I shall ne'er see more.

As I was mounted on the platform high,
My aged father was standing by;
My aged father did me deny,
And the name he gave me was the Croppy Boy.

It was in Dungannon this young man died,
And in Dungannon his body lies;
And you good Christians that do pass by
Just drop a tear for the Croppy Boy.

LIMERICK IS BEAUTIFUL

Michael Scanlan

Oh! Limerick is beautiful,
As everybody knows,
And by that City of my heart,
How proud the Shannon flows!
It sweeps down by the brave old town,
As pure in depth and tone,
As when Sarsfield drove the Saxon
From the walls of Garryowen.

'Tis not for Limerick that I sigh;
I love her in my soul;
The times may change and men will die,
And men will not control.
No! not for friends long passed away,
Or days for ever flown,
But that the maiden I adore
Is sad in Garryowen.

The girl I love is beautiful,
And world-wide is her fame,
She dwells down by the rushing tide
And Eire is her name.

And dearer than my very life,
Her glances are to me,
The light that guides my stormy soul
Across Life's stormy sea.

I loved her in my boyhood,
And now in manhood's bloom,
The vision of my life is still
To dry thy tears, aroon;
I'd sink into the tomb, or dance
Beneath the gallows tree,
To see her and her hills, once more,
Proud, passionate and free.

GORTNAMONA

Percy French

Long, long ago in the woods of Gortnamona,
I thought the birds were singing in the blackthorn tree;
But oh! it was my heart that was ringing, ringing, ringing,
With the joy that you were bringing O my love, to me.

Long, long, ago, in the woods of Gortnamona,
I thought the wind was sighing round the blackthorn tree;
But oh! it was the banshee that was crying, crying, crying,
And I knew my love was dying far across the sea.

Now if you go through the woods of Gortnamona,
You hear the raindrops creeping through the blackthorn tree.
But oh! it is the tears I am weeping, weeping, weeping,
For the loved one that is sleeping far away from me.

THE WEARIN' O' THE GREEN

Traditional

O Paddy dear, an' did ye hear the news that's goin' round?
The shamrock is by law forbid to grow on Irish ground!
No more Saint Patrick's Day we'll keep, his colour can't be seen,
For there's a cruel law agin the wearin' o' the Green!
I met wid Napper Tandy, and he took me by the hand,
And he said, 'How's poor ould Ireland, and how does she stand?'
She's the most disthressful country that iver yet was seen,
For they're hangin' men an' women there for the wearin' o' the
Green.

And if the colour we must wear is England's cruel Red,
Let it remind us of the blood that Ireland has shed;
Then pull the shamrock from your hat, and throw it on the sod,
And never fear, 'twill take root there, tho' under foot 'tis trod!
When the law can stop the blades of grass from growin' as they
grow,
And when the leaves in summer-time their colour dare not show,
Then I will change the colour, too, I wear in my caubeen,
But 'till that day, plase God, I'll stick to wearin' o' the Green.

THE IRISH DRAGOON

Charles O'Malley

Oh love is the soul of an Irish dragoon,
In battle, in bivouac, or in saloon –
From the tip of his spur to his bright sabretasche.

With his soldierly gait and his bearing so high,
His gay laughing look, and his light speaking eye,
He frowns at his rival, he ogles his wench,
He springs in his saddle and 'chasses' the French,
With his jingling spur and his bright sabretasche.

His spirits are high, and he little knows care,
Whether sipping his claret, or charging a square –
With his jingling spur and his bright sabretasche.
As ready to sing or to skirmish he's found,
To take off his wine, or take up his ground;
When the bugle may call him, how little he fears,
To charge forth in column, and beat the Mounseers –
With his jingling spur and his bright sabretasche.

When the battle is over, he gaily rides back
To cheer every soul in the night bivouac –
With his jingling spur and his bright sabretasche.
Oh, there you may see him in full glory crown'd
As he sits 'mid his friends on the hardly won ground,
And hear with what feeling the toast he will give,
As he drinks to the land where all Irishmen live
With his jingling spur and his bright sabretasche.

THE MEN OF THE WEST

William Rooney

While ye honour in song and in story
The names of the patriot men,
Whose valour has covered with glory
Full many a mountain and glen,
Forget not the boys of the heather,
Who marshalled their bravest and best,
When Eire was broken in Wexford,
And looked for revenge to the West!
I give you 'The gallant old West,' boys,
Where rallied our bravest and best
When Ireland was broken and bleeding,
Hurrah for the men of the West!

The hilltops with glory were flowing,
'Twas the eve of a bright harvest day,
When the ships we'd been wearily waiting
Sailed into Killala's broad bay;
And over the hills went the slogan,
To waken in every breast
The fire that has never been quenched, boys,
Among the true hearts of the West.
I give you 'The gallant old West,' boys,
Where rallied our bravest and best
When Ireland was broken and bleeding,
Hurrah for the men of the West!

Killala was ours ere the midnight,
And high over Ballina town,
Our banners in triumph were waving
Before the next sun had gone down;

We gathered to speed and good work, boys,
The true men anear and afar;
And history can tell how we routed
The redcoats thro' old Castlebar,
I give you 'The gallant old West,' boys,
Where rallied our bravest and best
When Ireland was broken and bleeding,
Hurrah for the men of the West!

And pledge me 'The stout sons of France,' boys,
Bold Humbert and all his brave men,
Whose tramp, like the trumpet of battle,
Brought hope to the drooping again.
Since Eire has caught to her bosom
On many a mountain and hill
The gallants who fell so they're here, boys,
To cheer us to Victory still.
I give you 'The gallant old West,' boys,
Where rallied our bravest and best
When Ireland was broken and bleeding,
Hurrah for the men of the West!

Though all the bright dreamings we cherished
Went down in disaster and woe,
The spirit of old still is with us
That never would bend to the foe;
And Connacht is ready whenever
The loud rolling tuck of the drum
Rings out to awaken the echoes
And tell us the morning has come.
So here's to the gallant old West, boys,
That rallied her bravest and best,
When Ireland was broken and bleeding,
Hurrah, boys! Hurrah for the West!

DANNY BOY

Traditional

Oh Danny boy, the pipes the pipes are calling,
From glen to glen and down the mountain side,
The Summer's gone and all the flowers are dying,
'Tis you 'tis you must go and I must bide.

But come you back when Summer's in the meadow,
Or when the valley's hushed and white with snow,
'Tis I'll be there in sunshine or in shadow,
Oh Danny boy, oh Danny boy, I love you so.

And if you come when all the flowers are dying,
And I am dead, as dead I well may be,
You'll come and find the place where I am lying,
And kneel and say an 'Ave' there for me.

And I shall hear, tho' soft you tread above me,
And all my dreams will warm and sweeter be,
If you will not fail to tell me that you love me,
Then I shall sleep in peace, until you come to me.

KELLY OF KILLANN

(A Ballad of 'Ninety-Eight')
P. J. McCall

What's the news? What's the news? O my bold Shelmalier,
With your long-barrelled gun of the sea?

Say what wind from the sun blows his messenger here
With a hymn of the dawn for the free?
'Goodly news, goodly news, do I bring you from Forth;
For the Boys march at morn from the South to the North,
Led by Kelly, the Boy from Killann!'

'Tell me who is that giant with gold curling hair –
He who rides at the head of your band?
Seven feet is his height, with some inches to spare,
And he looks like a king in command!' –
'Ah, my lads, that's the Pride of the Bold Shelmaliers,
'Mong our greatest of heroes, a Man! –
Fling your beavers aloft and give three ringing cheers
For John Kelly, the Boy from Killann!'

Enniscorthy's in flames and old Wexford is won,
And the Barrow tomorrow we cross,
On a hill o'er the town we have planted a gun
That will batter the gateways of Ross!
All the Forth men and Bargy men march o'er the heath,
With brave Harvey to lead on the van;
But the foremost of all in the grim Gap of Death
Will be Kelly, the Boy from Killann.

But the gold sun of Freedom grew darkened at Ross,
And it set by the Slaney's red waves;
And poor Wexford, stript naked, hung high on a cross,
With her heart pierced by traitors and slaves!
Glory O! Glory O! to her brave sons who died
For the cause of long down-trodden man!
Glory O! to Mount Leinster's own darling and pride –
Dauntless Kelly, the Boy from Killann!

THE HARP THAT ONCE
THROUGH TARA'S HALLS

Thomas Moore

The harp that once through Tara's halls
    The soul of music shed,
Now hangs as mute on Tara's walls
    As if that soul were fled.
So sleeps the pride of former days,
    So glory's thrill is o'er,
And hearts, that once beat high for praise,
    Now feel that pulse no more.

No more to chiefs and ladies bright
    The harp of Tara swells;
The chord alone, that breaks at night,
    Its tale of ruin tells.
Thus Freedom now so seldom wakes,
    The only throb she gives,
Is when some heart indignant breaks,
    To show that still she lives.

GOD SAVE IRELAND

T. D. Sullivan

High upon the gallows tree swung the noble-hearted three,
By the vengeful tyrant stricken in their bloom;
But they met him face to face, with the spirit of their race,
And they went with soul undaunted to their doom.

'God Save Ireland,' said the heroes; 'God save Ireland,' said they
all,
'Whether on the scaffold high, or the battlefield we die
O, what matter when for Erin dear we fall!'

Girt around with cruel foes, still their courage proudly rose,
For they thought of hearts that loved them far and near,
Of the millions true and brave, o'er the ocean's swelling wave,
And the friends in holy Ireland ever dear.

    God save Ireland, etc.,

Climbed they up the rugged stair, rung their voices out in
prayer,
Then with England's fatal chord around them cast,
Close beside the gallows tree kissed like brothers lovingly,
True to home and faith and freedom to the last.

    God save Ireland etc.,

Never till the lastest day shall the memory pass away
Of the gallant lives thus given for our land;
But on the Cause must go, midst joy or weal or woe,
Till we've made our Isle a Nation free and grand.

    God save Ireland, etc.,

THE PEELER AND THE GOAT

Traditional

A Bansha Peeler wint won night
On duty and pathrollin' O,
An' met a goat upon the road,
And tuck her for a sthroller O.
Wud bay'net fixed he sallied forth,
An' caught her by the wizzen O,
An' then he swore a mighty oath,
'I'll send you off to prison O'.

'Oh, mercy, sir!' the goat replied,
'Pray let me tell my story O!
I am no rogue, no Ribbonman,
No Croppy, Whig, or Tory O;
I'm guilty not of any crime
Of petty or high thraison O,
I'm sadly wanted at this time,
For this is the milkin' saison O.'

'It is in vain for to complain
Or give your tongue such bridle O,
You're absent from your dwellin' place,
Disorderly and idle O.
Your hoary locks will not prevail,
Nor your sublime oration O,
You'll be thransported by Peel's Act,
Upon my information O.'

'No penal law did I transgress
By deeds or combination O.

41

I have no certain place to rest,
No home or habitation O.
But Bansha is my dwelling-place,
Where I was bred and born O.
Descended from an honest race,
That's all the trade I've learned O.'

'I will chastise your insolince
And violent behaviour O;
Well bound to Cashel you'll be sint,
Where you will gain no favour O.
The magistrates will all consint
To sign your condemnation O;
From there to Cork you will be sint
For speedy thransportation O.'

'This parish an' this neighbourhood
Are paiceable and thranquil O;
There's no disturbance here, thank God!
An' long may it continue so,
I don't regard your oath a pin,
Or sign for my committal O,
My jury will be gintlemin
And grant me my acquittal O.'

'The consequince be what it will,
A Peeler's power I'll let you know,
I'll handcuff you, at all events,
And march you off to Bridewell O.
An' sure, you rogue, you can't deny
Before the judge or jury O,
Intimidation with your horns,
An' threatening me with fury O.'

'I make no doubt but you are dhrunk,
Wud whiskey, rum, or brandy O,
Or you wouldn't have such gallant spunk
To be so bould or manly O.
You readily would let me pass
If I had money handy O,
To thrate you to a potheen glass –
Oh! it's then I'd be the dandy O.'

THE SOUTH DOWN MILITIA

Traditional

O Boys, it was fine, when in battle we did join
Along with good King Billy at the Battle of the Boyne.
Says James: 'I'll take the first train home: it's more than I can
stand,
For the South Down Militia is the terror of the land!'

CHORUS
You may talk about your Queen's Guards, Scots Greys and
all,
You may rave about your Kilties and your gallant Forty-
twa,
Or any other regiment under the King's command,
But the South Down Militia is the terror of the land!

When we went up to London, in September, '62,
The King and Queen and Dukes were there, parading for review,
'Oh blood an' thunder!' says the Queen, as she waved her lily-
white hand,
'Sure, the South Down Militia is the terror of the land!'

CHORUS

When Kruger heard the regiment was landed at Cape Town
'De Wet', says he, 'we're bet,' says he, 'they've sent out the
South Down;
And De Wet, my boyo, that is true, we'll have to leave the Rand,
For the South Down Militia is the terror of the land!'

CHORUS

When we went out to Flanders to fight the awful Hun,
The Kaiser said to old Von Kluck: 'The war is nearly done!
I never thought the Orange Drum would beat the German Band
Oh! the South Down Militia is the terror of the land!'

CHORUS

When the Sultan heard the regiment was at the Dardanelles,
He rushed out of his harem and he gave the three awful yells –
'Allah! Allah save us, save us or be damned!
For the South Down Militia is the terror of the land!'

CHORUS

THE ROSE OF TRALEE

Traditional

The pale moon was rising above the green mountain,
The sun was declining beneath the blue sea,
When I stray'd with my love to the pure crystal fountain,
That stands in the beautiful vale of Tralee;

She was lovely and fair as the Rose of the summer,
Yet 'twas not her beauty alone that won me,
Oh! no! 'twas the truth in her eyes ever dawning
That made me love Mary, the Rose of Tralee.

The cool shades of ev'ning their mantle were spreading,
And Mary all smiling was list'ning to me,
The moon thro' the valley her pale rays was shedding
When I won the heart of the Rose of Tralee;
Though lovely and fair as the Rose of the summer,
Yet 'twas not her beauty alone that won me,
Oh, no! 'twas the truth in her eyes ever dawning
That made me love Mary, the Rose of Tralee.

THE FLOWER OF FINAE

Thomas Davis

Bright red is the sun on the waves of Lough Sheelin,
A cool gentle breeze from the mountains is stealing,
While fair round its islets the small ripples play
But fairer than all is the Flower of Finae.

Her hair is like night and her eyes like grey morning,
She trips on the heather as if its touch scorning,
Yet her heart and her lips are as mild as May-day,
Sweet Eily MacMahon, the Flower of Finae.

But who down the hillside than red deer runs fleeter,
And who on the lakeside is hastening to greet her?
Who but Fergus O'Farrell, the fiery and gay,
The darling and pride of the Flower of Finae.

One kiss and one clasp, and one wild look of gladness;
Ah! why do they change on a sudden to sadness?
He has told his hard fortune, no more he can stay,
He must leave his poor Eily to pine at Finae.

For Fergus O'Farrell was true to his sireland
And the dark hand of tyranny drove him from Ireland;
He joins the Brigade in the wars far away,
But he vows he'll come back to the Flower of Finae.

He fought at Cremona – she hears of his story;
He fought at Cassona – she's proud of his glory,
Yet sadly she sings 'Shule Aroon' all the day,
'Oh, come, come my darling, come home to Finae'.

Eight long years have passed till she's nigh broken-hearted,
Her 'reel' and her 'rock' and her 'flax' she has parted;
She sails with the 'Wild Geese' to Flanders away,
And leaves her sad parents alone in Finae.

Lord Clare on the field of Ramillies is charging,
Before him the Sassanach squadrons enlarging,
Behind him the Cravats their sections display,
Beside him rides Fergus and shouts for Finae.

On the slopes of La Judoigne the Frenchmen are flying
Lord Clare and his squadrons the foe still defying,
Outnumbered and wounded retreat in array:
And bleeding, rides Fergus, and thinks of Finae.

In the cloister of Ypres a banner is swaying,
And by it a pale weeping maiden is praying,
That flag's the sole trophy of Ramillies' fray,
The nun is poor Eily, the Flower of Finae.

OH BAY OF DUBLIN

Lady Dufferin

Oh! Bay of Dublin, my heart you're troubling;
Your beauty haunts me like a fever drame,
Like frozen fountains that the sun sets bubbling
My heart's blood warms when I but hear your name;
And never till this life pulse ceases
My earliest thought you'll cease to be;
Oh! there's no one here knows how fair that place is,
And no one cares how dear it is to me.

Sweet Wicklow mountains! The sunlight sleeping
On your green banks is a picture rare,
You crowd around me, like young girls peeping,
And puzzling me to say which is most fair.
As tho' you'd see your own sweet faces,
Reflected in that smooth and silver sea,
Oh! my blessin' on these lovely places,
Tho' no one cares how dear they are to me.

How often when at work I'm sitting,
And musing sadly on the days of yore,
I think I see my Katy knitting,
And the children playing round the cabin door;
I think I see the neighbours' faces
All gather'd round, their long lost friend to see,
Oh! tho' no one knows how fair that place is,
Heaven knows how dear my poor home was to me.

COME BACK, PADDY REILLY

Percy French

The Garden of Eden has vanished they say,
But I know the lie of it still.
Just turn to the left at the bridge of Finea,
And stop when half-way to Coote hill.
'Tis there I will find it, I know sure enough,
When fortune has come to my call.
Oh, the grass it is green around Ballyjamesduff,
And the blue sky is over it all!
And tones that are tender and tones that are gruff
Are whispering over the sea,
'Come back, Paddy Reilly, to Ballyjamesduff,
Come home, Paddy Reilly, to me.'

My mother once told me that when I was born,
The day that I first saw the light,
I looked down the street on that very first morn
And gave a great crow of delight.
Now most new-born babies appear in a huff
And start with a sorrowful squall,
But I knew I was born in Ballyjamesduff
And that's why I smiled on them all!
The baby's a man now, he's toil-worn and tough,
Still, whispers come over the sea,
'Come back, Paddy Reilly, to Ballyjamesduff,
Come home, Paddy Reilly, to me.'

The night that we danced by the light o' the moon,
Wid Phil to the fore wid his flute,
When Phil threw his lip over 'Come agin soon',
He'd dance the foot out o'yer boot!

The day that I took long Magee by the scruff,
For slanderin' Rosie Kilrain:
Then marchin' him straight out of Ballyjamesduff,
Assisted him into a drain.
Oh! sweet are me dreams as the dudeen I puff,
Of whisperings over the sea:
'Come back, Paddy Reilly, to Ballyjamesduff,
Come home, Paddy Reilly, to me.'

I've loved the young women of every land,
That always come easy to me;
Just barrin' the belles of the Blackamore brand,
And the chocolate shapes of Feegee.
But that sort of love is a moonshining stuff,
And never will addle me brain;
For bells will be ringin' in Ballyjamesduff
For me and me Rosie Kilrain;
And all through their glamour, their gas, and their guff,
A whisper comes over the sea:
'Come back, Paddy Reilly, to Ballyjamesduff,
Come home, Paddy Reilly, to me.'

BOULAVOGUE

P. J. McCall

At Boulavogue, as the sun was setting
O'er bright May meadows of Shelmalier,
A rebel hand set the heather blazing
And brought the neighbours from far and near.
Then Father Murphy, from old Kilcormack,
Spurred up the rocks with a warning cry;

'Arm! Arm!' he cried, 'for I've come to lead you,
For Ireland's freedom we fight or die.'

He led us on 'gainst the coming soldiers,
The cowardly Yeomen we put to flight;
'Twas at the Harrow the boys of Wexford
Showed Bookey's regiment how men could fight.
Look out for hirelings, King George of England,
Search every kingdom where breathes a slave,
For Father Murphy of the County Wexford
Sweeps o'er the land like a mighty wave.

We took Camolin and Enniscorthy,
And Wexford storming drove out our foes;
'Twas at Slieve Coillte our pikes were reeking
With the crimson stream of the beaten Yeos
At Tubberneering and Ballyellis
Full many a Hessian lay in his gore;
Ah, Father Murphy, had aid come over,
The green flag floated from shore to shore!

At Vinegar Hill, o'er the pleasant Slaney,
Our heroes vainly stood back to back,
And the Yeos at Tullow took Father Murphy
And burned his body upon the rack.
God grant you glory, brave Father Murphy,
And open Heaven to all your men;
The cause that called you may call tomorrow
In another fight for the green again.

WHISTLIN' PHIL McHUGH

Percy French

Oh! Whistlin' Phil McHugh,
Has come over from Bunlaghy,
An' we don't know what's come to
Little Mary Ann Mulcahy,
For ever since the day
That Phil he came a whistlin',
She stands in the doorway
An' she's waitin' and she's listenin'.

CHORUS
Oh! Mary you're contrary,
Come in and shut the door;
Phil's a rover, sure 'tis over,
And he'll not come back, asthore.
But she's listenin' for the whistlin'
And she's waitin' by the shore,
For that arrum to be warum,
Round her waist once more.

There's Thady of the Cows,
Sure you know 'Ten-acre Thady',
Wid his fine new slated house,
He'd make her quite the lady,
But Thady needn't stay,
And there's no use his inthragin',
For her heart is far away
'Tis wid Phil McHugh stravagin'.

CHORUS

There's Danny Michael Dan,
Who is six fut in his stockin's,
A very proper man,
But she never heeds his knockin's,
She'll keep him standin' there
For three quarthers of a minit,
But she's racin' like a hare
When she thinks that Phil is in it.

CHORUS

'Tis wisdom's golden rule
I do teach her till I tire,
That every girl's a fool,
Ay, and every man's a liar.
What's that, you say, you hear,
That's set you all thrimbly?
'Tis but the wind, I fear,
That is whistlin' down the chimbly.

CHORUS

Oh! Mary you're contrary,
Come in and bar the door;
What's that scuffin'?
Phil, you ruffian!
Sure I knew he'd come, asthore.
She's been settin' there and frettin'
But now her grievin's o'er;
And the singin' will be ringin'
In her heart once more!

MEMORY OF THE DEAD

John Kells Ingram, LL.D.

Who fears to speak of Ninety-Eight?
Who blushes at the name?
When cowards mock the patriot's fate,
Who hangs his head for shame?
He's all a knave or half a slave
Who slights his country thus:
But true men, like you men,
Will fill your glass with us.

We drink the memory of the brave
The faithful and the few –
Some lie far off beyond the wave,
Some sleep in Ireland, too;
All, all are gone – but still lives on
The fame of those who died;
All true men, like you men,
Remember them with pride.

Some on the shores of distant lands
Their weary hearts have laid,
And by the stranger's heedless hands
Their lonely graves were made;
But, though their clay be far away,
Beyond the Atlantic foam,
In true men, like you men,
Their spirit's still at home.

The dust of some is Irish earth;
Among their own they rest;

And the same land that gave them birth
Has caught them to her breast;
And we will pray that from their clay
Full many a race may start
Of true men, like you men,
To act as brave a part.

They rose in dark and evil days
To right their native land;
They kindled here a living blaze
That nothing shall withstand;
Alas! that Might can vanquish Right –
They fell and passed away;
But true men, like you, men,
Are plenty here to-day.

Then here's their memory – may it be
For us a guiding light,
To cheer our strife for liberty,
And teach us to unite!
Through good and ill, be Ireland's still,
Though sad as theirs your fate;
And true men, be you men,
Like those of Ninety-Eight.

OFT, IN THE STILLY NIGHT

Thomas Moore

Oft, in the stilly night,
    Ere Slumber's chain has bound me,
Fond Memory brings the light
    Of other days around me;
        The smiles, the tears,
        Of boyhood's years,
    The words of love then spoken;
        The eyes that shone,
        Now dimmed and gone,
    The cheerful hearts now broken!
Thus, in the stilly night,
    Ere Slumber's chain hath bound me,
Sad Memory brings the light
    Of other days around me.

When I remember all
    The friends, so linked together,
I've seen around me fall,
    Like leaves in wintry weather;
        I feel like one,
        Who treads alone
    Some banquet-hall deserted,
        Whose lights are fled,
        Whose garlands dead,
    And all but he departed!
Thus, in the stilly night,
    Ere Slumber's chain has bound me,
Sad Memory brings the light
    Of other days around me.

KEVIN BARRY

Traditional

In Mountjoy Jail, one Monday morning,
High upon the gallows tree,
Kevin Barry gave his young life
For the cause of liberty.
But a lad of eighteen summers,
Yet no one can deny,
As he walked to death that morning
He proudly held his head on high.

Just before he faced the hangman
In his dreary prison cell,
British soldiers tortured Barry
Just because he would not tell
The names of his brave companions,
And other things they wished to know
'Turn informer or we'll kill you!'
Kevin Barry answered 'No!'

Calmly standing to attention,
While he bade his last farewell
To his broken-hearted mother,
Whose sad grief no one can tell.
For the cause he proudly cherished
This sad parting had to be;
Then to death walked, softly smiling,
That old Ireland might be free.

Another martyr for old Ireland,
Another murder for the Crown,

Whose brutal laws may kill the Irish,
But can't keep their spirit down.
Lads like Barry are no cowards,
From the foe they will not fly;
Lads like Barry will free Ireland,
For her sake they'll live and die.

DEAR OLD IRELAND

T. D. Sullivan

Deep in Canadian woods we've met,
From one bright island flown;
Great is the land we tread, but yet
Our hearts are with our own.
And ere we leave this shanty small,
While fades the Autumn day:
>   We'll toast old Ireland,
>   Dear old Ireland,
>   Ireland, boys, hurra!

We've heard her faults a hundred times,
The new ones and the old,
In songs and sermons, rants and rhymes,
Enlarged some fifty-fold.
But take them all, the great and small,
And this we've got to say:
>   Here's dear old Ireland!
>   Good old Ireland!
>   Ireland, boys, hurra!

We know that brave and good men tried
To snap her rusty chain –

That patriots suffered, martyrs died,
And all, 'tis said, in vain;
But no, boys, no! a glance will show
How far they've won their way –
 Here's good old Ireland!
 Loved old Ireland!
 Ireland, boys, hurra!

We've seen the wedding and the wake,
The patron and the fair;
And lithe young frames at the dear old games
In kindly Irish air;
And the loud 'hurroo', we have heard it, too,
And the thundering 'clear the way!'
 Here's gay old Ireland!
 Dear old Ireland!
 Ireland, boys, hurra!

And well we know, in the cool, grey eyes,
When the hard day's work is o'er,
How soft and sweet are the words that greet
The friends that meet once more;
With 'Mary, machree!' 'My Pat! 'tis he!'
And 'My own heart, night and day!'
 Ah! fond old Ireland!
 Dear old Ireland!
 Ireland, boys, hurra!

And happy and bright are the groups that pass
From their peaceful homes, for miles
O'er fields, and roads, and hills, to Mass,
When Sunday morning smiles!
And deep the zeal their true hearts feel
When low they kneel and pray.

Oh, dear old Ireland!
Blest old Ireland!
Ireland, boys, hurra!

But deep in Canadian woods we've met,
And we never may see again
That dear old isle where our hearts are set,
And our first fond hopes remain!
But, come, fill up another cup,
And with every cup let's say:
Here's loved old Ireland!
Good old Ireland!
Ireland, boys, hurra!

THE RISING OF THE MOON

Traditional

Air: The Wearing of the Green

'Oh! then tell me, Sean O'Farrell, tell me why you hurry so?'
'Hush, a bhuachaill, hush and listen,' and his cheeks were all
aglow.
'I bear orders from the Captain, get you ready quick and soon,
For the pikes must be together at the rising of the moon.'

'Oh! then tell me, Sean O'Farrell, where the gathering is to be?'
'In the old spot by the river, right well known to you and me.
One word more – for signal token – whistle up the marching
tune,
With your pike upon your shoulder, by the rising of the moon.'

Out from many a mudwall cabin eyes were watching through
the night,
Many a manly breast was throbbing for the blessed warning
light,
Murmurs passed along the valley like the banshee's lonely croon,
And a thousand blades were flashing at the rising of the moon.

There beside the singing river that dark mass of men were seen,
Far above the shining weapons hung their own immortal green,
'Death to every foe and traitor! Forward! Strike the marching
tune,
And, hurrah, my boys, for freedom! 'tis the rising of the moon.'

Well they fought for poor old Ireland and full bitter was their
fate –
Oh! what glorious pride and sorrow fills the name of Ninety-
Eight –
Yet, thank God, while hearts are beating in manhood's burning
noon
We will follow in their footsteps at the rising of the moon!

THE MAID OF SLIEVENAMON

Charles J. Kickham

Alone, all alone, by the wave-wash'd strand,
And alone in the crowded hall;
The hall it is gay, and the waves they are grand,
But my heart is not here at all;
It flies far away, by night and by day,
To the times and the joys that are gone;
And I never can forget the maid I met
In the valley near Slievenamon.

It was not the grace of her queenly air,
Nor her cheek of the rose's glow,
Nor her soft black eyes, nor her flowing hair,
Nor was it her lily-white brow.
'Twas the soul of truth, and of melting ruth,
And the smile like a summer dawn,
That stole my heart away one soft summer day,
In the valley near Slievenamon.

In the festive hall, by the star-watch'd shore,
My restless spirit cries:
'My love, oh, my love, shall I ne'er see you more;
And, my land, will you ne'er uprise?'
By night and by day, I ever, ever pray,
While lonely my life flows on,
To see our flag unrolled, and my true love to enfold,
In the valley near Slievenamon.

A NATION ONCE AGAIN

Thomas Davis

When boyhood's fire was in my blood,
I read of ancient freemen,
For Greece and Rome who bravely stood,
Three hundred men, and three men;
And then I prayed I yet might see
Our fetters rent in twain,
And Ireland, long a province, be
A Nation Once Again.

CHORUS:

    A Nation Once Again!
    A Nation Once Again!
    And Ireland, long a province, be
    A Nation Once Again.

And from that time, through wildest woe,
That hope had shone, a far light;
Nor could love's brightest summer glow
Outshine the solemn starlight;
It seemed to watch above my head
In forum, field and fane;
Its angel voice sang round my bed
A Nation Once Again!

Chorus

It whispered, too, that freedom's ark
And service high and holy,
Would be profaned by feelings dark
And passions vain and lowly:
For freedom comes from God's right hand
And needs a godly train;
And righteous men must make our land
A Nation Once Again.

Chorus

So, as I grew from boy to man,
I bent me to that bidding –
My spirit of each selfish plan
And cruel passion ridding;
For, this I hoped some day to aid –
Oh! can such a hope be vain?
When my dear country shall be made
A Nation Once Again.

Chorus

INDEX OF FIRST LINES